JOY-ANN REID

LIFE STORY

We strongly believe that this biography book will enlighten you in every way possible about this notable figure.

THIS IS THE TIME TO READ AND LEARN ABOUT GREAT PEOPLE

➢ Understand now that isolation is deadly and could prevent you from growing. You need to learn from great people.

➢ Be diligent and meticulous and you study the content in this book.

- ➢ **Ensure that you do not let go of the great things you learn from this book.**

- ➢ **Allow your impressions and ideas to let loose in the note section.**

- ➢ **Understand that this is reality and achievements of fellow humans.**

DAY ONE OF LEARNING

ALL YOU SHOULD START KNOWING NOW

If

Joy-Ann Reid is a well-known author, political analyst, and journalist who has made substantial contributions to the media and journalism fields. Her life narrative is one of tenacity, grit, and a strong desire for equality and social justice. Joy-Ann Reid was born in Brooklyn, New York, on December 8, 1968, into a family that placed a high importance on education, labor, and volunteerism. Her parents cultivated in her a strong sense of civic duty and a dedication to changing the world for the better.

MORE INFO

Joy-Ann Reid demonstrated an early interest in politics and current affairs. Her passion for writing and her love of reading inspired her to seek a career in journalism. Reid started her journalism career after earning a degree in visual and environmental studies from Harvard University. She worked for a number of newspapers, including the South Florida Sun-Sentinel and the Miami Herald.

<u>DAY TWO OF LEARNING</u>

ALL YOU SHOULD START KNOWING NOW

If

Joy-Ann Reid has gained recognition over her career for her perceptive analysis, razor-sharp humor, and daring take on difficult subjects. She has written about a broad variety of subjects, including pop culture, entertainment, politics, and social justice. Her ability to captivate audiences and start thought-provoking discussions has won her a devoted following and made her a respected voice in the media.

MORE INFO

Joy-Ann Reid began working with MSNBC in 2014 as a national correspondent and the host of the weekend program "AM Joy." Reid's unique blend of comedy and intelligence, together with his in-depth analysis of current events and dynamic conversations with guests, helped the show quickly gain popularity. In her role as host of "AM Joy," Reid has addressed some of the most important contemporary issues, including as immigration, healthcare, race relations, and climate change.

DAY THREE OF LEARNING

ALL YOU SHOULD START KNOWING NOW

If

Joy-Ann Reid is not just a television writer but also a prolific book. Among the works she has authored is "The Man Who Sold America: Trump and the Unraveling of the American Story," a critical examination of the Trump administration's effects on democracy in the United States. Reid is known for writing with insight, clarity, and a dedication to the truth.

MORE INFO

In addition to her career achievements, Joy-Ann Reid is a devoted supporter of equality and social justice. She has advocated for causes impacting underrepresented groups, such as immigrants, people of color, and LGBTQ people, using her platform. Reid has devoted her life to advancing inclusivity, empathy, and understanding through her writing, speaking engagements, and community involvement.

DAY FOUR OF LEARNING

ALL YOU SHOULD START KNOWING NOW

If

Joy-Ann Reid has experienced difficulties both personally and professionally in the last few years. She has been the victim of internet abuse and intimidation because of her strong opinions and criticism of influential people. Reid has persevered in her resolve to speak truth to power and defend her convictions in the face of these challenges.

MORE INFO

Considering the future, Joy-Ann Reid has a promising and exciting future ahead of her. She will surely have a lasting influence on anyone who have the opportunity to hear her voice as she advocates for social change and makes waves in the media. Her life narrative serves as an inspiration to the strength of tenacity, bravery, and moral rectitude in the face of difficulty.

DAY FIVE OF LEARNING

ALL YOU SHOULD START KNOWING NOW

If

n summary, Joy-Ann Reid's life narrative is one of empowerment and inspiration. Reid has persevered through hardships with poise and persistence, from her modest upbringing in Brooklyn to her ascent to fame as a reputable journalist and pundit. She is an inspiration to everyone who aspires to change the world because of her unshakable dedication to social justice, equality, and the sharing of the truth. Joy-Ann Reid's legacy will survive as a tribute to the strength of resiliency and enthusiasm in bringing about positive change, as she continues to shatter barriers and question conventions.

MORE INFO

In recent years, Joy-Ann Reid has had to navigate a difficult and complex environment on both a personal and professional level. Reid, a well-known journalist and pundit, has come under heavy fire for her candid opinions and daring reporting on current affairs.

DAY SIX OF LEARNING

ALL YOU SHOULD START KNOWING NOW

If

Reid has faced severe threats and attacks in the age of social media and internet abuse, frequently as a result of her criticisms of influential people and organizations. Reid has persevered in her resolve to speak truth to power and promote equality and social justice in the face of these obstacles.

MORE INFO

Joy-Ann Reid has personally struggled with the demands of being a well-known person in a politically divisive and increasingly divisive environment. Her high-profile position at MSNBC, where she presents the weekend program "AM Joy," has made her adept at navigating the media's fast-paced, constantly-evolving environment. Reid has clearly had many challenges in juggling her obligations as a professional with her personal life and wellbeing, as she works to uphold her honesty and integrity in the face of severe criticism.

DAY SEVEN OF LEARNING

ALL YOU SHOULD START KNOWING NOW

If

Joy-Ann Reid has had to deal with personal conflicts and setbacks in addition to the external pressures she encounters. Like many people in the spotlight, Reid has had to face her own flaws and vulnerabilities in addition to the pressure of other people's expectations and judgment. Reid's readiness to be open and sincere about her own experiences has been an inspiration to others and a source of strength in a society that frequently prizes authenticity over vulnerability.

MORE INFO

Joy-Ann Reid still has a big influence in the media and other fields in spite of these obstacles. Her commitment to elevating underrepresented perspectives, confronting structural injustices, and fostering compassion and understanding has brought her a devoted fan base and cemented her place as a reliable voice in the media. Reid has motivated numerous people to stand out for what they believe in and strive toward a more just and equitable society through her writing, speaking engagements, and advocacy activities.

Considering the future, The future holds a lot of promise and opportunity for Joy-Ann Reid. Reid is dedicated to using her platform for good and changing the world, even as she continues to manage the challenges of her personal and professional lives. Her steadfast commitment to social justice, equality, and the telling of the truth provides hope to those who work to bring about constructive change in their communities and beyond.

WE ARE HAPPY AND PROUD OF YOU!

- WE ARE OVERJOYED TO LEARN THAT YOU HAVE COMPLETED THIS BIOGRAPHY BOOK.

- Do not squander your newly acquired information; rather, put it to good use.

- Donating copies is a great way to show

THAT YOU CARE BECAUSE IT ALLOWS OTHER PEOPLE TO IMPROVE THEIR LIFE AS WELL.

www.ingramcontent.com/pod-product-compliance
Lightning Source LLC
LaVergne TN
LVHW050553270225
804698LV00008B/576